Wings
& *things*

Publications International, Ltd.
www.pilcookbooks.com

Microwave Cooking: Microwave ovens vary in wattage. Use the cooking times as guidelines and check for doneness before adding more time.

Preparation/Cooking Times: Preparation times are based on the approximate amount of time required to assemble the recipe before cooking, baking, chilling or serving. These times include preparation steps such as measuring, chopping and mixing. The fact that some preparations and cooking can be done simultaneously is taken into account. Preparation of optional ingredients and serving suggestions is not included.

Publications International, Ltd.
www.pilcookbooks.com

CONTENTS

All **AMERICAN**

Cranberry-Barbecue Chicken Wings

3 pounds chicken wings
   Salt and black pepper
1 jar (12 ounces)
   cranberry-orange
   relish
½ cup barbecue sauce
2 tablespoons quick-
   cooking tapioca
1 tablespoon prepared
   mustard

Slow Cooker Directions

1. Preheat broiler. Rinse chicken wings under cold water; pat dry with paper towels. Remove and discard wing tips. Cut each wing in half at joint. Place chicken on rack of broiler pan; season with salt and pepper.

2. Broil 4 to 5 inches from heat 10 to 12 minutes or until browned, turning once. Transfer chicken to slow cooker.

3. Stir relish, barbecue sauce, tapioca and mustard in small bowl. Pour over chicken. Cover; cook on LOW 4 to 5 hours.   *Makes 6 to 8 servings*

Prep Time: 20 minutes • Cook Time: 4 to 5 hours

TIP

Wings are just the thing for a summer backyard bash or a casual game day get-together. Do a quick count of your guests and plan on having 4 to 6 wings per person.

Tangy Baked Wings

1 pouch **CAMPBELL'S®
Dry Onion Soup and
Recipe Mix**

⅓ **cup honey**

2 **tablespoons spicy-brown
mustard**

18 **chicken wings (about
3 pounds)**

1. Stir the soup mix, honey and mustard with a spoon in a large bowl.

2. Cut the chicken wings at the joints into 54 pieces. Discard the tips or save for another use. Put the wings in the bowl. Toss to coat with the soup mixture. Place the wings on a large shallow-sided baking pan.

3. Bake at 400°F. for 45 minutes or until the wings are cooked through, turning halfway during cooking.

Makes 36 appetizers

Prep Time: 15 minutes • Bake Time: 45 minutes

Roasted Rosemary Chicken

¼ **cup finely chopped
onion**

2 **tablespoons butter,
melted**

1 **tablespoon chopped
fresh rosemary leaves
or 1 teaspoon dried
rosemary**

2 **cloves garlic, minced**

½ **teaspoon salt**

¼ **teaspoon black pepper**

4 **chicken leg quarters**

¼ **cup white wine or
chicken broth**

1. Preheat oven to 375°F.

2. Combine onion, butter, rosemary, garlic, salt and pepper in small bowl. Run finger under chicken skin to loosen. Rub onion mixture under and over skin. Place chicken, skin side up, in small shallow roasting pan. Pour wine over chicken.

3. Roast chicken 50 to 60 minutes or until chicken is browned and cooked through (165°F), basting often with pan juices.

Makes 4 servings

Jerk Wings with Ranch Dipping Sauce

½ cup mayonnaise

½ cup plain yogurt or sour cream

1½ teaspoons salt, divided

1¼ teaspoons garlic powder, divided

½ teaspoon black pepper, divided

¼ teaspoon onion powder

2 tablespoons orange juice

1 teaspoon sugar

1 teaspoon dried thyme

1 teaspoon paprika

¼ teaspoon ground nutmeg

¼ teaspoon ground red pepper

2½ pounds chicken wings

1. Preheat oven to 450°F. Spray baking sheet with nonstick cooking spray.

2. For dipping sauce, combine mayonnaise, yogurt, ½ teaspoon salt, ¼ teaspoon garlic powder, ¼ teaspoon black pepper and onion powder in small bowl. Cover; refrigerate until ready to serve.

3. Combine orange juice, sugar, thyme, paprika, nutmeg, red pepper, remaining 1 teaspoon salt, 1 teaspoon garlic powder and ¼ teaspoon black pepper in medium bowl.

4. Rinse chicken wings under cold water; pat dry with paper towels. Remove and discard wing tips. Cut each wing in half at joint. Add chicken to orange juice mixture; toss to coat.

5. Transfer chicken to prepared pan. Bake 25 to 30 minutes or until chicken is cooked through and skin is crisp. Serve with dipping sauce.

Makes 4 to 6 servings

Angel Wings

1 can (10¾ ounces)
condensed tomato
soup, undiluted

¾ cup water

¼ cup packed brown sugar

2½ tablespoons balsamic
vinegar

2 tablespoons chopped
shallots

2 pounds chicken wings

Slow Cooker Directions

1. Combine soup, water, brown sugar, vinegar and shallots in slow cooker; mix well.

2. Add chicken wings; stir to coat with sauce. Cover; cook on LOW 5 to 6 hours or until cooked through.

Makes 4 to 6 servings

Hot & Spicy Buffalo Chicken Wings

1 can (15 ounces)
DEL MONTE®
Original Recipe
Sloppy Joe Sauce

¼ cup thick and chunky
salsa, medium

1 tablespoon red wine
vinegar or cider
vinegar

20 chicken wings
(about 4 pounds)

1. Preheat oven to 400°F.

2. Combine sloppy joe sauce, salsa and vinegar in small bowl. Remove ¼ cup sauce mixture to serve with cooked chicken wings; cover and refrigerate. Set aside remaining sauce mixture.

3. Arrange wings in single layer in large, shallow baking pan; brush wings with remaining sauce mixture.

4. Bake chicken, uncovered, on middle rack in oven 35 minutes or until chicken is no longer pink in center, turning and brushing with remaining sauce mixture after 15 minutes. Serve with reserved ¼ cup sauce. Garnish, if desired. *Makes 4 servings*

Prep Time: 5 minutes • Cook Time: 35 minutes

Garlicky Gilroy Chicken Wings

1 cup olive oil, plus
   additional to
   grease pan

2 pounds chicken wings

2 heads fresh garlic,
   separated into cloves
   and peeled*

1 teaspoon hot pepper
   sauce, or to taste

1 cup grated Parmesan
   cheese

1 cup Italian-style bread
   crumbs

1 teaspoon black pepper

Ranch dip and celery
   slices (optional)

*To peel whole heads of garlic, drop
into boiling water for 5 to 10 seconds.
Immediately remove garlic with slotted
spoon. Plunge garlic into cold water;
drain. Peel away skins.

1. Preheat oven to 375°F. Grease 13×9-inch nonstick baking pan with oil.

2. Rinse chicken wings under cold water; pat dry with paper towels. Remove and discard wing tips. Cut each wing in half at joint.

3. Place 1 cup oil, garlin and hot pepper sauce in food processor; process until smooth. Pour garlic mixture into small bowl. Combine cheese, bread crumbs and black pepper in shallow dish. Dip chicken, one at a time, into garlic mixture, then roll in crumb mixture, coating evenly and shaking off excess.

4. Arrange chicken in single layer in prepared pan. Drizzle remaining garlic mixture over chicken; sprinkle with remaining crumb mixture. Bake 45 to 60 minutes or until chicken is browned and cooked through. Serve with ranch dip and celery slices if desired.

Makes 4 to 6 servings

TIP

Always thaw frozen chicken in the refrigerator because thawing poultry at room temperature increases the risk of bacteria formation. Allow poultry approximately 5 hours per pound to thaw.

Salsa-Style Wings

1½ pounds chicken wings
2 cups prepared salsa
¼ cup brown sugar

1. Preheat oven to 350°F. Line 13×9-inch baking pan with foil; place chicken in even layer in pan.

2. Stir salsa and brown sugar in medium bowl; pour over chicken.

3. Bake 1 hour or until chicken is cooked through, basting every 10 minutes with salsa mixture.

4. Serve with remaining salsa mixture.

Makes 3 to 4 servings

Grilled Chicken Thighs

8 boneless, skinless chicken thighs
3 tablespoons MRS. DASH® Chicken Grilling Blends™
4 tablespoons red wine vinegar
2 tablespoons tomato paste
2 tablespoons honey
1 to 2 tablespoons water

Lay chicken thighs side-by-side in large glass casserole. Score each thigh 2 to 3 times using sharp knife.

Combine Mrs. Dash® Chicken Grilling Blends™, vinegar, tomato paste, honey and water. Set aside ¼ cup. Pour remaining marinade over chicken; marinate in refrigerator at least 1 hour.

Preheat grill to medium heat.

Brush thighs with reserved marinade and grill 10 minutes on each side.

Makes 4 servings

Prep Time: 5 minutes • Cook Time: 20 minutes

Game-Winning Drumsticks

15 chicken drumsticks
(about 4 pounds)

1¾ cups SWANSON® Chicken Stock

½ cup Dijon-style mustard

⅓ cup Italian-seasoned dry bread crumbs

1. Put the chicken in a single layer in a 15×10-inch disposable foil pan.

2. Stir the stock and mustard in a small bowl. Pour the stock mixture over the chicken and turn to coat. Sprinkle the bread crumbs over the chicken. Cover the pan and refrigerate for 4 hours.

3. Bake at 375°F. for 1 hour or until the chicken is cooked through. Serve hot or at room temperature.

Makes 6 servings

Kitchen Tip: Keep disposable foil pans on hand to conveniently tote casseroles to friends' parties or covered dish suppers. As a safety reminder, be sure to support the bottom of the filled pan when placing them in and out of the oven.

Prep Time: 10 minutes • Marinate Time: 4 hours • Bake Time: 1 hour

Buffalo Chicken Wings

24 chicken wings

1 teaspoon salt

¼ teaspoon ground black pepper

4 cups vegetable oil for frying

¼ cup butter or margarine

¼ cup hot pepper sauce

1 teaspoon white wine vinegar

Celery sticks

1 bottle (8 ounces) blue cheese dressing

Cut tips off wings at first joint; discard tips. Cut remaining wings into two parts at the joint; sprinkle with salt and pepper. Heat oil in deep fryer or heavy saucepan to 375°F. Add half the wings; fry about 10 minutes or until golden brown and crisp, stirring occasionally. Remove with slotted spoon; drain on paper towels. Repeat with remaining wings.

Melt butter in small saucepan over medium heat; stir in pepper sauce and vinegar. Cook until thoroughly heated. Place wings on large platter. Pour sauce over wings. Serve warm with celery and dressing for dipping.

Makes 24 appetizers

Favorite recipe from **National Chicken Council**

Honey-Mustard Chicken Wings

3 pounds chicken wings

I teaspoon salt

I teaspoon black pepper

½ cup honey

½ cup barbecue sauce

2 tablespoons spicy brown mustard

I clove garlic, minced

3 to 4 thin lemon slices

Slow Cooker Directions

1. Preheat broiler. Rinse chicken wings under cold water; pat dry with paper towels. Remove and discard wing tips. Cut each wing in half at joint. Sprinkle with salt and pepper. Place chicken on broiler rack. Broil 4 to 5 inches from heat 10 minutes, turning halfway through cooking time. Place in slow cooker.

2. Combine honey, barbecue sauce, mustard and garlic in small bowl; mix well. Pour sauce over chicken. Top with lemon slices. Cover; cook on LOW 4 to 5 hours.

3. Remove and discard lemon slices. Serve wings with sauce from slow cooker.   *Makes 6 to 8 servings*

Prep Time: 20 minutes • Cook Time: 4 to 5 hours

Garlicky Chicken Wings

2 pounds TYSON® Fresh Chicken Wings

½ teaspoon salt

I tablespoon butter or margarine

I tablespoon olive oil

6 cloves garlic, chopped

¼ teaspoon crushed red pepper flakes

1. Preheat oven to 425°F. Spray 13×9-inch baking pan with nonstick cooking spray. Wash hands. Sprinkle chicken with salt. Wash hands.

2. Melt butter with olive oil in large skillet over medium-high heat. Add chicken; cook, turning occasionally, 10 minutes or until browned. Add garlic; cook and stir 1 minute longer. Stir in red pepper flakes; mix well.

3. Transfer chicken mixture to baking pan. Bake, turning once, 20 to 25 minutes or until internal juices of chicken run clear. (Or insert instant-read meat thermometer into thickest part of chicken. Temperature should read 180°F.) Refrigerate leftovers immediately.   *Makes 4 servings*

Serving Suggestion: Serve wings with olive salad and pepperoncini.

Prep Time: 5 minutes • Cook Time: 35 minutes

Original Buffalo Chicken Wings

Zesty Blue Cheese Dip (page 90)

2½ pounds chicken wings, split and tips discarded

½ cup *Frank's*® *RedHot*® Original Cayenne Pepper Sauce (or to taste)

⅓ cup butter or margarine, melted

Celery sticks

1. Prepare Zesty Blue Cheese Dip.

2. Deep fry* wings at 400°F 12 minutes or until crisp and no longer pink; drain.

3. Combine *Frank's RedHot* Sauce and butter in large bowl. Add wings to sauce; toss well to coat evenly. Serve with Zesty Blue Cheese Dip and celery.

Makes 24 to 30 individual pieces

Or prepare wings using one of the cooking methods below. Add wings to sauce; toss well to coat evenly.

To Bake: Place wings in single layer on rack in foil-lined roasting pan. Bake at 425°F 1 hour or until crisp and no longer pink, turning once halfway through baking time.

To Broil: Place wings in single layer on rack in foil-lined roasting pan. Broil 6 inches from heat 15 to 20 minutes or until crisp and no longer pink, turning once halfway through cooking time.

To Grill: Place wings on oiled grid. Grill over medium heat 30 to 40 minutes or until crisp and no longer pink, turning often.

Shanghai Red Wings: Cook chicken wings as directed above. Combine ¼ cup soy sauce, 3 tablespoons honey, 3 tablespoons *Frank's RedHot* Sauce, 2 tablespoons peanut oil, 1 teaspoon grated peeled fresh ginger and 1 teaspoon minced garlic in small bowl. Mix well. Pour sauce over wings; toss well to coat evenly.

Cajun Wings: Cook chicken wings as directed above. Combine ⅓ cup *Frank's RedHot* Sauce, ⅓ cup ketchup, ¼ cup (½ stick) melted butter or margarine and 2 teaspoons Cajun seasoning in small bowl. Mix well. Pour sauce over wings; toss well to coat evenly.

Santa Fe Wings: Cook chicken wings as directed above. Combine ¼ cup (½ stick) melted butter or margarine, ¼ cup *Frank's RedHot* Sauce, ¼ cup chili sauce and 1 teaspoon chili powder in small bowl. Mix well. Pour sauce over wings; toss well to coat evenly.

Appetizer Chicken Wings

2½ to 3 pounds (12 to 14) chicken wings

1 cup (8 ounces) fat-free French dressing

½ cup KARO® Light or Dark Corn Syrup

1 package (1.4 ounces) French onion soup, dip and recipe mix

1 tablespoon Worcestershire sauce

Cut tips from wings and discard. Cut wings apart at joints and arrange in 13×9×2-inch baking pan lined with foil.

In medium bowl mix dressing, corn syrup, recipe mix and Worcestershire sauce; pour over wings.

Bake in 350°F oven 60 minutes, stirring once, or until wings are tender. *Makes 24 servings*

Prep Time: 15 minutes • Cook Time: 60 minutes

Island Chicken Wings

8 TYSON® Individually Frozen Chicken Wings

1 can (4 ounces) diced green chiles, drained

¼ cup chopped onion

¼ cup golden raisins

2 tablespoons apricot preserves

1 tablespoon packed brown sugar

1 tablespoon lemon juice

¼ teaspoon ground allspice

1 large banana, peeled and cut into chunks

1 tablespoon garlic oil

Salt and black pepper, to taste

1. Wash hands. Cut off wing tips; discard or save for other purposes. Cut remaining wings apart at joints to make 2 pieces each. Wash hands.

2. Combine chiles, onion, raisins, preserves, brown sugar, lemon juice, allspice and banana in blender; purée until smooth.

3. Heat garlic oil in large skillet over medium-low heat. Season wings with salt and pepper to taste. Cook 18 to 20 minutes or until well-browned and internal juices of chicken run clear. (Or insert instant-read meat thermometer into thickest part of chicken. Temperature should read 180°F.)

4. Meanwhile, pour sauce into small saucepan and cook, stirring frequently, over medium heat 10 minutes to thicken liquid. Season with salt and pepper to taste. Serve with dipping sauce. Refrigerate leftovers immediately. *Makes 8 servings*

Tip: For additional flavor, marinate chicken wings in Italian dressing and then grill or broil.

Prep Time: 15 minutes • Cook Time: 20 minutes • Total Time: 35 minutes

Buffalo Chicken Drumsticks

8 chicken drumsticks

3 tablespoons hot pepper
sauce

1 tablespoon vegetable oil

1 clove garlic, minced

¼ cup mayonnaise

3 tablespoons sour cream

1 tablespoon white wine
vinegar

¼ teaspoon sugar

⅓ cup (about 1½ ounces)
crumbled blue cheese

2 cups hickory chips

Celery sticks

1. Place chicken in large resealable food storage bag. Combine hot pepper sauce, oil and garlic in small bowl; pour over chicken. Seal bag; turn to coat. Marinate in refrigerator at least 1 hour, or for hotter flavor, up to 24 hours, turning occasionally.

2. For blue cheese dressing, combine mayonnaise, sour cream, vinegar and sugar in another small bowl. Stir in cheese; cover and refrigerate until serving.

3. Prepare grill for direct cooking. Meanwhile, cover hickory chips with cold water; soak 20 minutes. Drain chicken, discarding marinade. Drain hickory chips; sprinkle over coals. Place chicken on grid over medium-high heat. Grill, covered, 25 to 30 minutes or until chicken is cooked through (165°F), turning occasionally. Serve with blue cheese dressing and celery sticks. *Makes 4 servings*

Hot Wings with Creamy Cool Dipping Sauce

Creamy Cool Dipping
Sauce (page 89)

¼ cup chopped onion

2 tablespoons olive oil

2 cloves garlic, minced

1½ cups barbecue sauce

2 to 3 teaspoons hot
pepper sauce

4 pounds chicken wings

1. Prepare grill for direct cooking.

2. Prepare Creamy Cool Dipping Sauce; set aside.

3. Place onion, oil and garlic in medium microwavable bowl. Microwave on HIGH 1½ to 2 minutes or until onion is tender. Add barbecue sauce and hot pepper sauce; stir until blended. Set aside.

4. Grill chicken, covered, over medium-high heat 25 minutes or until chicken is cooked through, turning after 15 minutes. Turn and brush with barbecue sauce mixture frequently during last 5 minutes of cooking. Serve with Creamy Cool Dipping Sauce.

Makes 8 to 10 servings

Hot 'n' Honeyed Chicken Wings

1 cup PACE® Picante Sauce

¼ cup honey

½ teaspoon ground ginger

12 chicken wings *or* chicken drummettes

1. Stir the picante sauce, honey and ginger in a small bowl.

2. Cut the chicken wings at the joints into 24 pieces. Discard the tips or save them for another use. Put the wings in a small bowl. Add the picante sauce mixture and toss to coat. Put the wings on a foil-lined shallow baking pan.

3. Bake at 400°F. for 55 minutes or until the wings are glazed and cooked through,* turning and brushing often with sauce during the last 30 minutes of cooking.

Makes 24 appetizers

*The internal temperature of the chicken should reach 170°F.

Prep Time: 10 minutes • Bake Time: 55 minutes

Sweet Hot Chicken Wings

3 pounds chicken wings

¾ cup salsa, plus additional for serving

⅔ cup honey

⅓ cup soy sauce

¼ cup Dijon mustard

2 tablespoons vegetable oil

1 tablespoon grated fresh ginger

½ teaspoon *each* grated lemon and orange peel

1. Rinse chicken wings under cold water; pat dry with paper towels. Remove and discard wing tips. Cut each wing in half at joint. Place wings in 13×9-inch baking dish.

2. Combine salsa, honey, soy sauce, mustard, oil, ginger, lemon peel and orange peel in small bowl; mix well. Pour over chicken. Cover; marinate in refrigerator at least 6 hours or overnight.

3. Preheat oven to 400°F. Line 15×10-inch jelly-roll pan with foil. Place chicken in single layer on prepared pan. Pour marinade evenly over chicken. Bake 40 to 45 minutes or until chicken is browned and cooked through. Serve warm with additional salsa.

Makes 6 to 8 servings

Nutty Oven-Fried Chicken Drumsticks

12 chicken drumsticks
1 egg, beaten
1 cup cornflake crumbs
1/3 cup finely chopped pecans
1 tablespoon sugar
1 1/2 teaspoons salt
1/2 teaspoon onion powder
1/2 teaspoon black pepper
1/4 cup (1/2 stick) butter or margarine, melted

1. Preheat oven to 400°F. Line baking sheet with foil. Toss chicken legs with egg to coat.

2. Combine cornflake crumbs, pecans, sugar, salt, onion powder and pepper in large resealable food storage bag. Add chicken to crumb mixture, two pieces at a time; shake to coat.

3. Place chicken on prepared baking sheet; drizzle with butter. Bake 40 to 45 minutes or until cooked through (165°F). *Makes 6 servings*

TIP

It is much easier to chop nuts if they are warmed up a bit first. Heat them in the oven at 325°F for about 5 minutes or in the microwave on HIGH for 2 to 3 minutes.

Chicken Wings in Cerveza

1½ pounds chicken wings or drumettes*

1 teaspoon salt

1 teaspoon dried thyme

⅛ teaspoon black pepper

1 bottle (12 ounces) Mexican beer

*When using drumettes, simply place them in the marinade without cutting.

1. Rinse chicken wings under cold water; pat dry with paper towels. Remove and discard wing tips. Cut each wing in half at joint. Place chicken in shallow bowl; sprinkle with salt, thyme and pepper. Pour beer over chicken; toss to coat. Cover; marinate in refrigerator 2 hours or up to 6 hours.

2. Preheat oven to 375°F. Line shallow baking pan with foil; spray with nonstick cooking spray.

3. Drain chicken, reserving marinade. Arrange chicken in single layer on prepared pan. Bake 40 minutes or until chicken is browned on all sides and cooked through, turning and basting with reserved marinade occasionally. *Do not brush with marinade during last 5 minutes of baking.* Discard remaining marinade.

Makes 3 to 4 servings

BBQ Orange Wings

8 TYSON® Individually Frozen Chicken Wings

½ cup bottled barbecue sauce

½ cup orange marmalade, or plum or pineapple preserves

Salt and black pepper, to taste

1. Preheat oven to 400°F. Line 13×9-inch baking pan with foil; spray with nonstick cooking spray. Wash hands. Arrange frozen wings in single layer in pan. Combine barbecue sauce and marmalade; reserve half of mixture to serve with cooked wings. Wash hands.

2. Bake wings 20 minutes; drain and discard juices. Sprinkle wings with salt and pepper. Bake an additional 20 minutes. Turn over wings and baste with sauce. Bake 15 to 20 minutes more or until internal juices of chicken run clear. (Or insert instant-read meat thermometer into thickest part of chicken. Temperature should read 180°F.)

3. Heat reserved sauce and serve with wings. Refrigerate leftovers immediately.   *Makes 4 servings*

Prep Time: 5 minutes • Cook Time: 1 hour

Soy-Braised Chicken Wings

2½ pounds chicken wings

¼ cup dry sherry

¼ cup soy sauce

3 tablespoons sugar

2 tablespoons cornstarch

2 tablespoons minced
garlic, divided

2 teaspoons red pepper
flakes

12 chicken wings (about
2½ pounds), tips
removed and cut
into halves

2 tablespoons vegetable
oil

3 green onions, cut into
1-inch pieces

¼ cup chicken broth

1 teaspoon sesame oil

1 tablespoon sesame
seeds, toasted*

To toast sesame seeds, place in small skillet. Shake skillet over medium-low heat about 3 minutes or until seeds begin to pop and turn golden.

1. Rinse chicken wings under cold water; pat dry with paper towels. Remove and discard wing tips. Cut each wing in half at joint.

2. Combine sherry, soy sauce, sugar, cornstarch, 1 tablespoon garlic and pepper flakes in large bowl; mix well. Reserve ¼ cup marinade. Add chicken to bowl. Cover; marinate in refrigerator overnight, turning once or twice.

3. Drain chicken; discard marinade. Heat wok or deep skillet over high heat 1 minute. Add 1 tablespoon vegetable oil; heat 30 seconds. Add half of chicken; cook 5 to 10 minutes or until chicken is browned. Remove with slotted spoon to clean bowl. Repeat with remaining oil and chicken.

4. Add remaining 1 tablespoon garlic and green onions to wok; cook and stir 30 seconds. Add chicken and broth. Cover; cook 5 to 10 minutes or until chicken is cooked through, stirring occasionally.

5. Add sesame oil to reserved marinade; mix well. Pour over chicken in wok; cook and stir 2 minutes or until chicken is glazed with marinade. Transfer to serving platter; sprinkle with sesame seeds.

Makes 4 to 6 servings

Mahogany Wings

I can (10½ ounces)
   CAMPBELL'S®
   Condensed Beef Broth

2 bunches green onions,
   chopped

I cup soy sauce

I cup plum sauce

6 cloves garlic, minced

½ cup light molasses or
   honey

¼ cup cider vinegar

6 pounds chicken wings

I tablespoon cornstarch

1. Stir the broth, onions, soy sauce, plum sauce, garlic, molasses and vinegar in a 6-quart slow cooker removable insert.*

2. Cut off the chicken wing tips and discard. Cut the chicken wings in half at the joint. Add the chicken to the cooker and stir to coat. Cover and refrigerate for 6 hours or overnight.

3. Stir ½ cup of the marinade and cornstarch in small bowl. Stir into the chicken mixture.

4. Cover and cook on HIGH for 4 to 5 hours** or until the chicken is cooked through.

Makes 18 servings

*If your slow cooker doesn't have a removable insert, you can stir the marinade ingredients into a large bowl instead. Add the chicken and stir to coat. Cover and refrigerate as directed. Pour the chicken mixture into the cooker and proceed with Steps 3 and 4 as directed.

**Or on LOW for 7 to 8 hours.

Ginger-Garlic Barbecued Turkey Wings

4 turkey wings

Ginger-Garlic Sauce
   2 tablespoons light soy
      sauce

   2 tablespoons dry sherry

   I tablespoon fresh
      gingerroot, finely
      chopped

   I teaspoon canola oil

   I teaspoon brown sugar

   I clove garlic, minced

1. Discard wing tips and divide wings into 2 pieces.

2. In large saucepan, cover turkey with water and bring to a boil. Simmer for 20 minutes.

3. Meanwhile, combine remaining ingredients to make Ginger-Garlic Sauce, stirring well to dissolve the sugar.

4. Remove turkey from water, and place in sauce to marinate in refrigerator for 2 to 12 hours.

5. Remove wings from sauce and grill over medium heat for 20 to 30 minutes, turning often.

Makes 4 servings

Favorite recipe from **National Turkey Federation**

Oriental Chicken Wings

3 pounds chicken wings

1 cup chopped red onion

1 cup soy sauce

¾ cup packed light brown sugar

¼ cup dry sherry

2 tablespoons chopped fresh ginger

2 cloves garlic, minced

Chopped fresh chives (optional)

Slow Cooker Directions

1. Preheat broiler. Line baking sheet with foil.

2. Rinse chicken wings under cold water; pat dry with paper towels. Remove and discard wing tips. Cut each wing in half at joint. Transfer chicken to prepared baking sheet. Broil chicken about 5 minutes per side. Transfer to slow cooker.

3. Combine onion, soy sauce, brown sugar, sherry, ginger and garlic in large bowl until well blended. Pour over chicken in slow cooker.

4. Cover; cook on LOW 5 to 6 hours or on HIGH 2 to 3 hours. Sprinkle with chives, if desired.

Makes 6 to 8 servings

Grilled Tandoori-Style Chicken Wings with Cucumber-Yogurt Sauce

3 pounds chicken wings

Juice of 2 limes

2 tablespoons finely minced garlic

1 tablespoon finely minced fresh ginger

1 teaspoon kosher salt

1 teaspoon chili powder

1 teaspoon garam masala*

Cucumber-Yogurt Sauce (page 89)

*Garam masala is an Indian spice blend that can include black pepper, cinnamon, cloves, coriander, cumin, cardamom and other spices. It can be found in Indian markets and in the spice section of some supermarkets.

1. Rinse chicken wings under cold water; pat dry with paper towels. Remove and discard wing tips. Cut each wing in half at joint.

2. Combine lime juice, garlic, ginger, salt, chili powder and garam masala in small bowl. Rub paste evenly over chicken. Cover; marinate in refrigerator 2 to 4 hours.

3. Preheat outdoor grill or grill pan. Preheat oven to 350°F. Line baking sheet with foil. Grill chicken 7 to 10 minutes or until browned on all sides.

4. Transfer chicken to prepared baking sheet. Bake 35 to 40 minutes or until cooked through. Meanwhile, prepare Cucumber-Yogurt Sauce.

5. Serve chicken with Cucumber-Yogurt Sauce.

Makes 6 to 8 servings

Ginger-Lime Chicken Thighs

⅓ cup vegetable oil

3 tablespoons lime juice

3 tablespoons honey

2 teaspoons grated fresh ginger *or* 1 teaspoon ground ginger

¼ to ½ teaspoon red pepper flakes

6 boneless skinless chicken thighs

1. Combine oil, lime juice, honey, ginger and pepper flakes in small bowl. Pour ½ cup marinade into large resealable food storage bag. Add chicken. Seal bag; turn to coat. Marinate in refrigerator 30 to 60 minutes, turning occasionally.

2. Prepare grill for direct cooking.

3. Remove chicken from marinade; discard marinade. Grill chicken over medium-high heat 12 minutes or until chicken is cooked through, turning once. Brush with remaining marinade during last 5 minutes of cooking.   *Makes 4 to 6 servings*

Grilled Vietnamese-Style Chicken Wings

3 pounds chicken wings or drumettes

⅓ cup honey

¼ to ⅓ cup sliced lemongrass

¼ cup fish sauce

2 tablespoons chopped garlic

2 tablespoons minced shallots

2 tablespoons chopped fresh ginger

2 tablespoons lime juice

2 tablespoons canola oil

Chopped cilantro (optional)

1. Rinse chicken wings under cold water; pat dry with paper towels. Remove and discard wing tips. Cut each wing in half at joint.

2. Combine honey, lemongrass, fish sauce, garlic, shallots, ginger, lime juice and oil in food processor; process until smooth.

3. Pour marinade into large resealable food storage bag. Add chicken. Seal bag; turn to coat. Marinate in refrigerator 4 hours or overnight.

4. Preheat outdoor grill or grill pan. Preheat oven to 350°F. Line baking sheet with foil. Remove chicken from marinade; reserve marinade. Grill chicken 7 to 10 minutes or until browned, basting occasionally with marinade.

5. Transfer chicken to prepared baking sheet; bake 20 to 30 minutes or until cooked through. Sprinkle with cilantro.   *Makes 6 to 8 servings*

Chicken Drumettes with Chive-Caper Mayonnaise

⅓ cup mayonnaise

1 tablespoon minced chives

2 teaspoons capers

¼ teaspoon black pepper, divided

¼ cup all-purpose flour

½ teaspoon paprika, divided

¼ teaspoon salt

2 eggs

½ cup plain dry bread crumbs

1½ pounds chicken drumettes

2 tablespoons unsalted butter

2 tablespoons vegetable oil

1. Combine mayonnaise, chives, capers and ⅛ teaspoon pepper in small bowl. Cover; refrigerate until ready to serve.

2. Combine flour, ¼ teaspoon paprika, salt and remaining ⅛ teaspoon pepper in large resealable food storage bag. Beat eggs in large shallow bowl. Combine bread crumbs and remaining ¼ teaspoon paprika on large plate.

3. Rinse chicken wings under cold water; pat dry with paper towels. Add chicken to flour mixture; shake well to coat. Dip chicken in eggs, then roll in bread crumbs.

4. Heat butter and oil in large heavy skillet over medium-high heat until butter melts and mixture sizzles. Cook chicken in batches 6 minutes or until browned, turning once. Reduce heat to low. Cook chicken 5 minutes more or until cooked through, turning once. Serve with Chive-Caper Mayonnaise.

Makes 3 to 4 servings

Ginger Wings with Peach Dipping Sauce

Peach Dipping Sauce (page 88)

¼ cup soy sauce

2 cloves garlic, minced

1 teaspoon ground ginger

¼ teaspoon white pepper

2 pounds chicken wings

1. Preheat oven to 400°F. Line baking sheet with foil.

2. Prepare Peach Dipping Sauce; set aside. Combine soy sauce, garlic, ginger and pepper in large bowl.

3. Rinse chicken wings under cold water; pat dry with paper towels. Remove and discard wing tips. Cut each wing in half at joint. Add chicken to soy sauce mixture; stir until coated. Place chicken in single layer in prepared pan. Bake 40 to 50 minutes or until chicken is browned and cooked through, turning once. Serve with Peach Dipping Sauce.

Makes 4 to 6 servings

Asian Barbecue Skewers

2 pounds boneless skinless chicken thighs

½ cup soy sauce

⅓ cup packed brown sugar

2 tablespoons sesame oil

3 cloves garlic, minced

½ cup thinly sliced green onions (optional)

1 tablespoon toasted sesame seeds (optional)

Slow Cooker Directions

1. Cut each thigh into 4 (1½-inch-thick) pieces. Thread onto 7-inch wooden skewers, folding thinner pieces if necessary. Place skewers in 6-quart slow cooker, layering as flat as possible.

2. Combine soy sauce, brown sugar, oil and garlic in small bowl. Reserve ⅓ cup sauce; set aside. Pour remaining sauce over skewers. Cover; cook on LOW 2 hours. Turn skewers; cook 1 hour more.

3. Transfer skewers to serving platter. Discard cooking liquid. Pour reserved sauce over skewers; sprinkle with green onions and sesame seeds.

Makes 4 to 6 servings

Prep Time: 10 minutes • Cook Time: 3 hours

Bombay Chicken Wings

2 (1¼-pound) packages chicken wing drummettes (24 pieces)

1 teaspoon curry powder

½ teaspoon ground turmeric

2 tablespoons soy sauce

2 tablespoons vegetable oil

2 tablespoons minced green onion

2 cloves garlic, minced

⅛ teaspoon black pepper

Sprigs of cilantro for garnish

Yogurt Chutney Dipping Sauce (page 90)

In large bowl, mix all ingredients except chicken wings and cilantro to make marinade. Add chicken wings, making sure all pieces are coated well with mixture; cover and refrigerate for at least 1 hour.

Prepare Yogurt Chutney Dipping Sauce. Preheat oven to 360°F. Drain chicken wings; place in single layer on jelly-roll pan. Bake 25 minutes until golden brown. Arrange on platter surrounding a bowl of Yogurt Chutney Dipping Sauce. Garnish with cilantro sprigs and serve. *Makes 24 appetizers*

Favorite recipe from **National Chicken Council**

Thai Chicken Wings

1 tablespoon peanut oil

5 pounds chicken wings

½ cup coconut milk

1 tablespoon sugar

1 tablespoon Thai green curry paste

1 tablespoon fish sauce

¾ cup prepared spicy peanut sauce

Slow Cooker Directions

1. Rinse chicken wings under cold water; pat dry with paper towels. Remove and discard wing tips. Cut each wing in half at joint.

2. Heat oil in large nonstick skillet over medium-high heat. Add chicken and brown in several batches, about 6 minutes per batch. Transfer chicken to slow cooker.

3. Stir coconut milk, sugar, curry paste and fish sauce in small bowl until combined. Add to slow cooker. Cover; cook on LOW 6 to 7 hours or on HIGH 3 to 3½ hours. Drain cooking liquid. Stir in peanut sauce before serving.   *Makes 10 to 12 servings*

Prep Time: 20 minutes • Cook Time: 6 to 7 hours (LOW) or 3 to 3½ hours (HIGH)

West Indies Curried Drumsticks

12 chicken drumsticks

¾ teaspoon salt, divided

½ teaspoon paprika

1 tablespoon cornstarch

1 tablespoon sugar

1 cup orange juice

2 cloves garlic, crushed

1½ teaspoons curry powder

1 teaspoon grated orange peel

½ teaspoon ground ginger

½ cup chopped cashews

Place chicken in large baking dish; sprinkle with ½ teaspoon salt and paprika. Bake in 375°F oven 30 minutes. Mix cornstarch and sugar in small saucepan. Stir in orange juice, garlic, curry powder, orange peel, ginger and remaining ¼ teaspoon salt. Cook and stir over medium heat until mixture boils and thickens. Pour sauce over chicken; bake, basting once with pan juices, about 25 minutes more or until chicken is fork-tender. Sprinkle cashews over chicken.

Makes 6 servings

Favorite recipe from **Delmarva Poultry Industry, Inc.**

Chipotle Orange BBQ Drumsticks

½ cup barbecue sauce, preferably mesquite or hickory smoked

1 to 2 tablespoons minced canned chipotle peppers in adobo sauce

1 teaspoon grated orange peel

8 chicken drumsticks

1 teaspoon ground cumin

1. Prepare grill for direct cooking.

2. Combine barbecue sauce, chipotle peppers and orange peel in small bowl; set aside.

3. Sprinkle drumsticks evenly with cumin.

4. Grill chicken, covered, over medium-high heat 30 to 35 minutes or until cooked through (165°F), turning frequently. Baste with sauce during last 5 minutes of cooking, turning and basting frequently until all of sauce is used.   *Makes 4 to 6 servings*

Spicy Korean Chicken Wings

½ cup reduced-sodium soy sauce

¼ cup cider vinegar

¼ cup honey

¼ cup chili garlic sauce

2 tablespoons orange juice

1 tablespoon sesame oil

2 tablespoons peanut oil, plus additional for frying

2 tablespoons grated fresh ginger

3 pounds chicken wings or drumettes

Sesame seeds (optional)

1. Combine soy sauce, vinegar, honey, chili garlic sauce, orange juice and sesame oil in large bowl until blended. Heat 2 tablespoons peanut oil in medium skillet over medium-high heat. Add ginger; cook and stir 2 minutes. Add soy sauce mixture; cook and stir 2 minutes.

2. Heat 2 inches peanut oil in large heavy saucepan over medium-high heat until 350° to 375°F, adjusting heat to maintain temperature.

3. Rinse chicken wings under cold water; pat dry with paper towels. Remove and discard wing tips Cut each wing in half at joint.

4. Cook chicken 8 to 10 minutes or until crisp and browned and chicken is cooked through. Drain on paper towels.

5. Add chicken to sauce; toss to coat. Sprinkle with sesame seeds.   *Makes 6 to 8 servings*

Spicy Almond Chicken Drumettes

3 tablespoons vegetable oil

2 tablespoons jerk seasoning

½ teaspoon salt

3 pounds chicken drumettes

I cup slivered almonds, finely chopped

1. Combine oil, jerk seasoning and salt in small bowl; stir until blended. Place chicken in large bowl. Pour seasoning mixture over chicken; toss to coat. Cover; marinate in refrigerator 20 to 30 minutes.

2. Preheat oven to 400°F. Line shallow baking sheet with foil; spray with nonstick cooking spray.

3. Place almonds in shallow bowl. Roll chicken in almonds until coated. Place on prepared baking sheet. Bake 30 to 35 minutes or until chicken is cooked through.
Makes 6 to 8 servings

Maple and Honey Wheat Beer Glazed Chicken Thighs

I bottle (12 ounces) honey wheat beer, divided

⅔ cup orange juice, divided

¼ cup plus 2 tablespoons maple syrup, divided

2 tablespoons lemon juice

2 cloves garlic, minced

2 teaspoons grated fresh ginger, divided

6 chicken thighs

2 teaspoons cornstarch

2 teaspoons water

I¼ teaspoons salt

¼ teaspoon black pepper

1. Combine ¾ cup beer, ⅓ cup orange juice, 2 tablespoons maple syrup, lemon juice, garlic and I teaspoon ginger in large resealable food storage bag. Add chicken. Seal bag; turn to coat. Marinate in refrigerator 2 hours or overnight.

2. Combine remaining ¾ cup beer, ⅓ cup orange juice, ¼ cup maple syrup and I teaspoon ginger in small saucepan over medium-high heat. Bring to a boil; reduce heat to medium and simmer 4 minutes or until slightly thickened.

3. Whisk cornstarch and water in small bowl. Add cornstarch mixture, salt and pepper to saucepan; increase heat to high and boil I minute or until thickened. Remove from heat.

4. Prepare grill for indirect cooking. Remove chicken from marinade; discard marinade. Grill chicken skin side down 10 minutes. Turn and generously brush with glaze; grill 5 minutes. Repeat turning and brushing chicken 4 more times. Grill chicken 5 minutes more after last application of glaze or until cooked through (165°F).
Makes 4 to 6 servings

Moroccan-Spiced Chicken Wings

¼ cup orange juice

3 tablespoons tomato paste

2 teaspoons ground cumin

1 teaspoon salt

1 teaspoon curry powder

1 teaspoon ground turmeric

½ teaspoon ground cinnamon

½ teaspoon ground ginger

1 tablespoon olive oil

Slow Cooker Directions

1. Stir orange juice, tomato paste, cumin, salt, curry powder, turmeric, cinnamon and ginger in large bowl; set aside.

2. Rinse chicken wings under cold water; pat dry with paper towels. Remove and discard wing tips. Cut each wing in half at joint.

3. Heat oil in large nonstick skillet over medium-high heat. Add chicken and brown in several batches, about 6 minutes per batch. Transfer chicken to bowl with sauce; toss to coat.

4. Transfer chicken to slow cooker. Cover; cook on LOW 6 to 7 hours or on HIGH 3 to 3½ hours.

Makes 10 to 12 servings

Prep Time: 20 minutes • Cook Time: 6 to 7 hours (LOW) or 3 to 3½ hours (HIGH)

Gingered Chicken Thighs

1 tablespoon peanut or vegetable oil

½ teaspoon hot chili oil

8 chicken thighs

2 cloves garlic, minced

¼ cup sweet and sour sauce

1 tablespoon soy sauce

2 teaspoons minced fresh ginger

Cilantro and orange peel (optional)

1. Heat peanut oil and chili oil in large nonstick skillet over medium-high heat. Cook chicken, skin side down, 4 minutes or until golden brown. Reduce heat to low; turn chicken. Cover; cook 15 to 18 minutes or until cooked through (165°F). Drain fat.

2. Increase heat to medium. Add garlic; cook and stir 2 minutes. Combine sweet and sour sauce, soy sauce and ginger in small bowl. Brush half of mixture over chicken; turn and brush with remaining mixture. Cook 5 minutes or until sauce has thickened, turning once.

3. Transfer chicken to serving platter; pour sauce evenly over chicken. Garnish with cilantro and orange peel.

Makes 4 to 6 servings

Chicken Bites with Orange-Walnut Sauce

½ cup orange marmalade

3 tablespoons orange juice

2 tablespoons chopped walnuts

2 pitted prunes, chopped

1 tablespoon raisins

¼ teaspoon black pepper, divided

2 boneless skinless chicken breasts, cut into 1-inch cubes

Grated peel and juice of 1 orange

3 tablespoons olive oil, divided

2 tablespoons Spanish sherry

½ teaspoon salt

1. Combine marmalade, 3 tablespoons orange juice, walnuts, prunes, raisins and ⅛ teaspoon pepper in small microwavable bowl. Microwave on HIGH 1 minute; stir until blended.

2. Place chicken, orange peel, orange juice, 1 tablespoon oil, sherry, salt and remaining ⅛ teaspoon pepper in medium bowl; toss to coat.

3. Heat remaining 2 tablespoons oil in medium nonstick skillet over medium heat. Using slotted spoon, transfer chicken to skillet in two batches. Cook 5 minutes or until chicken is browned and cooked through. Add any remaining marinade. Bring to a boil; boil 1 minute. Transfer chicken and sauce to serving plate.   *Makes 4 to 6 servings*

Note: The sauce can be prepared, covered and refrigerated up to two days in advance. Allow sauce to come to room temperature before serving.

Marinated Thai Turkey Wings

4 turkey wings

Thai Marinade
½ cup smooth peanut butter

½ cup water

3 tablespoons light soy sauce

3 tablespoons fresh lemon juice

2 tablespoons brown sugar

2 green onions, chopped

3 drops hot pepper sauce

1. Discard wing tips and divide wings into 2 pieces.

2. In large saucepan, cover turkey with water and bring to a boil. Simmer for 20 minutes.

3. Meanwhile, combine remaining ingredients to make Thai Marinade, stirring well to dissolve sugar.

4. Remove turkey from water and place in marinade to marinate in refrigerator for 2 to 12 hours.

5. Remove wings from marinade and grill over medium heat for 20 to 30 minutes, turning often.

Makes 4 servings

Favorite recipe from **National Turkey Federation**

Coconut Chicken Tenders with Spicy Mango Salsa

1 firm ripe mango, peeled and chopped

½ cup chopped red bell pepper

3 tablespoons chopped green onions

2 tablespoons chopped fresh cilantro

Salt and ground red pepper

1½ cups flaked coconut

1 egg

1 tablespoon vegetable oil

¾ pound chicken tenders

1. Combine mango, bell pepper, green onions and cilantro in small bowl. Season to taste with salt and ground red pepper. Transfer half of salsa to food processor; process until finely chopped (almost puréed). Combine with remaining salsa.

2. Preheat oven to 400°F. Line baking sheet with foil. Spread coconut on prepared baking sheet; bake 5 minutes or until lightly browned, stirring every 2 minutes. Transfer coconut to food processor; process until finely chopped but not pasty. Remove to shallow bowl or plate.

3. Beat egg, oil and pinch of ground red pepper in small bowl. Add chicken; toss to coat. Roll chicken in coconut; transfer to same baking sheet. Bake 18 to 20 minutes or until chicken is cooked through. Serve with Spicy Mango Salsa. *Makes 2 to 3 servings*

Island Jerk Chicken Wings

1 cup Hawaiian barbecue sauce

1 can (6 ounces) crushed pineapple, drained

¼ cup packed brown sugar

2 tablespoons lime juice

1 clove garlic, chopped

½ teaspoon grated ginger

Hot pepper sauce (optional)

3 pounds chicken wings

2 tablespoons Caribbean jerk seasoning

1. Preheat oven to 350°F. Line baking sheet with foil.

2. Combine barbecue sauce, pineapple, brown sugar, lime juice, garlic, ginger and hot pepper sauce, if desired, in food processor; process until well blended.

3. Rinse chicken wings under cold water; pat dry with paper towels. Remove and discard wing tips. Cut each wing in half at joint.

4. Place chicken on prepared baking sheet; rub with jerk seasoning until well coated. Bake 20 minutes. Baste with sauce; bake 20 minutes more or until chicken is cooked through. *Makes 6 to 8 servings*

Bar **FOOD**

Portobello Mushroom Burgers

1 tablespoon olive oil,
   divided

¾ cup thinly sliced shallots

4 large portobello
   mushrooms, stems
   removed

⅛ teaspoon salt

⅛ teaspoon black pepper

2 cloves garlic, minced

¼ cup mayonnaise

2 tablespoons chopped
   basil

4 whole grain hamburger
   buns

4 ounces fresh mozzarella,
   cut into ¼-inch slices

2 roasted red bell peppers,
   cut into strips

1. Preheat broiler. Line baking sheet with foil.

2. Heat 1 teaspoon oil in medium saucepan over medium heat. Add shallots; cook and stir 6 to 8 minutes or until golden brown and soft. Set aside.

3. Drizzle mushrooms on both sides with remaining 2 teaspoons oil; season with salt and pepper. Place mushrooms gill side up on prepared baking sheet. Sprinkle evenly with garlic.

4. Broil mushrooms 4 minutes per side or until tender.

5. Combine mayonnaise and basil in small bowl until well blended. Spread both sides of each bun with basil mayonnaise. Top bottom halves of buns with shallots, mozzarella, mushroom and bell pepper strips; top with top halves of buns.   *Makes 4 burgers*

Three Pepper Quesadillas

1 cup *each* thin green, red and yellow bell pepper strips

½ cup thin onion slices

⅓ cup butter *or* margarine

½ teaspoon ground cumin

1 package (8 ounces) PHILADELPHIA® Cream Cheese, softened

1 package (8 ounces) KRAFT® Shredded Sharp Cheddar Cheese

10 TACO BELL® Home Originals®* Flour Tortillas

1 jar (16 ounces) TACO BELL® Home Originals®* Thick 'N Chunky Salsa

*TACO BELL® and HOME ORIGINALS® are registered trademarks owned and licensed by Taco Bell Corp.

PREHEAT oven to 425°F. Cook and stir peppers and onion in butter in large skillet on medium-high heat until crisp-tender. Stir in cumin. Drain, reserving liquid.

BEAT cream cheese and Cheddar cheese with electric mixer on medium speed until well blended. Spoon 2 tablespoons cheese mixture onto each tortilla; top each evenly with pepper mixture. Fold tortillas in half; place on ungreased baking sheet. Brush with reserved liquid.

BAKE 10 minutes or until heated through. Cut each tortilla into thirds. Serve warm with salsa.

Makes 30 servings (1 piece each)

Make Ahead: Prepare as directed except for baking; cover. Refrigerate. When ready to serve, bake, uncovered, at 425°F, 15 to 18 minutes or until heated through.

Prep Time: 20 minutes • Bake Time: 10 minutes

TIP

To soften cream cheese quickly, remove it from the wrapper and place it on a medium microwavable plate. Microwave on MEDIUM (50%) 15 to 20 seconds or until slightly softened.

Buffalo Chicken Tenders

3 tablespoons Louisiana-
   style hot sauce

½ teaspoon paprika

¼ teaspoon ground red
   pepper

1 pound chicken tenders

½ cup blue cheese dressing

¼ cup sour cream

2 tablespoons crumbled
   blue cheese

1 medium green or
   red bell pepper, cut
   lengthwise into
   ½-inch slices

1. Preheat oven to 375°F. Spray 11×7-inch baking dish with nonstick cooking spray. Combine hot sauce, paprika and ground red pepper in small bowl; brush over chicken. Place chicken in prepared dish. Cover; marinate in refrigerator 30 minutes.

2. Bake about 15 minutes or until chicken is cooked through.

3. Combine blue cheese dressing, sour cream and blue cheese in small bowl. Serve chicken with dip and bell pepper slices.   *Makes 4 to 6 servings*

Tex-Mex Potato Skins

3 hot baked potatoes, split
   lengthwise

¾ cup (3 ounces) shredded
   Cheddar or pepper
   Jack cheese

1⅓ cups *French's*® French
   Fried Onions, divided

¼ cup chopped green
   chilies

¼ cup crumbled cooked
   bacon

Salsa and sour cream

1. Preheat oven to 350°F. Scoop out inside of potatoes, leaving ¼-inch shells. Reserve inside of potatoes for another use.

2. Arrange potato halves on baking sheet. Top with cheese, *⅔ cup* French Fried Onions, chilies and bacon.

3. Bake 15 minutes or until heated through and cheese is melted. Cut each potato half crosswise into thirds. Serve topped with salsa, sour cream and remaining onions.   *Makes 18 servings*

Tip: To bake potatoes quickly, microwave at HIGH 10 to 12 minutes or until tender.

Variation: For added Cheddar flavor, substitute *French's*® Cheddar French Fried Onions for the original flavor.

Prep Time: 15 minutes • Cook Time: 15 minutes

Pork Tenderloin Sliders

2 tablespoons olive oil, divided

2 pork tenderloins (about 1 pound each)

2 teaspoons chili powder

¾ teaspoon ground cumin

½ teaspoon salt

½ teaspoon black pepper

12 green onions

½ cup mayonnaise

1 chipotle pepper in adobo sauce, minced

2 teaspoons lime juice

12 dinner rolls, sliced in half horizontally

12 slices Monterey Jack cheese

1. Prepare grill for direct cooking.

2. Rub 1 tablespoon oil evenly over tenderloins. Combine chili powder, cumin, salt and black pepper in small bowl. Sprinkle evenly over tenderloins, coating all sides. Place green onions and remaining 1 tablespoon oil in large resealable food storage bag; seal bag. Knead to coat onions with oil.

3. Combine mayonnaise, chipotle pepper and lime juice in small bowl until well blended. Cover and refrigerate until ready to serve.

4. Grill tenderloins, covered, 15 to 20 minutes or until cooked through (160°F), turning occasionally. Remove to cutting board. Tent with foil; let stand 10 minutes.

5. Meanwhile, grill green onions about 3 minutes or until browned, turning occasionally. Cool slightly; coarsely chop.

6. Thinly slice tenderloins. Spread chipotle mayonnaise on bottom halves of rolls. Top with green onions, tenderloin slices and cheese. Replace top halves of rolls. *Makes 12 sandwiches*

Buffalo-Style Chicken Nachos

2 cups diced cooked chicken

⅓ cup *Frank's*® *RedHot*® Original Cayenne Pepper Sauce

2 tablespoons melted butter

1 bag (10 ounces) tortilla chips

3 cups shredded Cheddar or Monterey Jack cheese

1. Preheat oven to 350°F. Combine chicken, *Frank's RedHot* Sauce and butter. Layer chips, chicken and cheese in ovenproof serving dish or baking dish.

2. Bake 5 minutes just until cheese melts. Garnish as desired. Splash on more *Frank's RedHot* Sauce to taste. *Makes 4 servings*

Prep Time: 5 minutes • Cook Time: 5 minutes

Taco Chili Fries

1 bag (16 ounces) frozen French fries

2 pounds lean ground beef

1½ cups water

2 packets (1.25 ounces each) ORTEGA® Taco Seasoning Mix

1 cup ORTEGA® Salsa, any variety

1 can (15 ounces) JOAN OF ARC® black beans, drained

1 can (6 ounces) sliced black olives, drained

1 can (4 ounces) ORTEGA® Diced Green Chiles

2 cups (8 ounces) shredded Cheddar cheese

1 cup sour cream (optional)

FOLLOW package directions for baking fries. Set aside.

BROWN ground beef in medium skillet over medium-high heat. Stir in water and seasoning mix. Cook 5 minutes. Remove from heat.

SPOON salsa, beans, olives, chiles, cheese and sour cream, if desired, into separate bowls. Place fries in large bowl near meat mixture and toppings. Using heat-resistant ceramic plates, allow guests to create their own chili fries with meat and toppings. (Reserve sour cream until after mixture has been broiled.)

PLACE ceramic plate under broiler about 4 minutes or until fries reheat and cheese melts. Top with sour cream, if desired. Serve immediately.

Makes 6 servings

Prep Time: 15 minutes • Start to Finish Time: 45 minutes

TIP

Try adding a variety of cheeses, from a jalapeño-Cheddar or Monterey Jack, to a stout blue cheese. Offer a selection of diced fresh vegetables to top chili fries.

One-Bite Burgers

1 package (11 ounces) refrigerated breadstick dough (12 breadsticks)

1 pound ground beef

2 teaspoons hamburger seasoning mix

9 slices Cheddar or American cheese, quartered (optional)

36 round dill pickle slices

Ketchup or mustard

1. Preheat oven to 375°F. Separate dough into 12 breadsticks; cut each breadstick into 3 equal pieces. Working with one piece at a time, tuck ends under to meet at center, pressing to seal and form very small bun about 1½ inches in diameter and ½ inch high.

2. Place buns seam side down on ungreased baking sheet. Bake 11 to 14 minutes or until golden brown. Remove to wire racks.

3. Meanwhile, combine beef and seasoning in large bowl. Shape into 36 patties, using about 2 teaspoons per patty.

4. Heat large skillet over medium heat. Cook patties 7 minutes or until cooked through, turning once. Top with cheese slice, if desired.

5. Split buns in half crosswise. Place patties on bottom halves of buns. Top with pickle slices, small dollops of ketchup or mustard and top halves of buns.

Makes 36 mini burgers

Raspberry-Balsamic Glazed Meatballs

1 bag (34 ounces) frozen fully cooked meatballs

1 cup raspberry preserves

3 tablespoons sugar

3 tablespoons balsamic vinegar

1½ tablespoons Worcestershire sauce

¼ teaspoon red pepper flakes

1 tablespoon grated fresh ginger (optional)

Slow Cooker Directions

1. Spray slow cooker with nonstick cooking spray. Add frozen meatballs.

2. Combine preserves, sugar, vinegar, Worcestershire sauce and pepper flakes in small microwavable bowl. Microwave on HIGH 45 seconds. Stir; microwave 15 seconds more or until melted (mixture will be chunky). Reserve ½ cup mixture. Pour remaining mixture over meatballs and toss to coat. Cover; cook on LOW 5 hours or on HIGH 2½ hours.

3. Turn slow cooker to HIGH. Sir in ginger, if desired, and reserved ½ cup preserves mixture. Cook, uncovered, 15 to 20 minutes or until slightly thickened, stirring occasionally. *Makes 4 servings*

Spicy Grilled Quesadillas

8 flour tortillas (8 inch)

2 cups shredded
   Cheddar cheese
   (about 8 ounces)

1 jar (16 ounces) PACE®
   Chunky Salsa

1 cup diced cooked
   chicken

4 medium green onions,
   chopped (about
   ½ cup)

   Vegetable oil

1 container (8 ounces)
   sour cream

1. Top each of 4 tortillas with ½ cup cheese, ¼ cup salsa, ¼ cup chicken and 2 tablespoons green onions. Brush the edges of the tortillas with water. Top with the remaining tortillas and press the edges to seal.

2. Lightly oil the grill rack and heat the grill to medium. Brush the tops of the quesadillas with oil. Place the quesadillas oil-side down on the grill rack. Brush the other side of the quesadillas with oil. Grill the quesadillas for 5 minutes or until the cheese is melted, turning the quesadillas over once during grilling. Remove the quesadillas from the grill and let stand 2 minutes.

3. Cut the quesadillas into wedges. Serve with the remaining salsa and sour cream.   *Makes 4 servings*

Kitchen Tip: Quesadillas are an easy way to turn leftover meat and shredded cheese into a whole new meal. You can even combine different varieties of shredded cheese to make the 2 cups needed in this recipe.

Serving Suggestion: Serve with Spanish-style rice and fresh carrot sticks. For dessert, serve fresh apple slices with prepared caramel sauce.

Prep Time: 10 minutes • Cook Time: 5 minutes • Stand Time: 2 minutes

Spinach, Crab and Artichoke Dip

1 package (10 ounces) frozen chopped spinach, thawed and squeezed nearly dry

1 package (8 ounces) cream cheese

1 jar (6 to 7 ounces) marinated artichoke hearts, drained and finely chopped

1 can (6½ ounces) crabmeat, drained and shredded

¼ teaspoon hot pepper sauce

Melba toast or whole grain crackers (optional)

Slow Cooker Directions

1. Combine spinach, cream cheese, artichoke hearts, crabmeat and hot pepper sauce in slow cooker.

2. Cover; cook on HIGH 1½ to 2 hours or until heated through, stirring after 1 hour. (Dip will stay warm in slow cooker for 2 hours.) Serve with melba toast, if desired. *Makes 10 servings*

Baked Sweet Potato Fries with Spicy Apricot Dipping Sauce

3 sweet potatoes (12 to 14 ounces each), peeled and cut into narrow wedges

2 tablespoons vegetable oil

1½ teaspoons kosher salt

¼ teaspoon black pepper

Spicy Apricot Dipping Sauce (page 87)

1. Preheat oven to 450°F. Gently toss potatoes, oil, salt and pepper in large bowl until evenly coated.

2. Divide potatoes between 2 large baking sheets or jelly-roll pans. Bake 30 minutes or until lightly browned.

3. Meanwhile, prepare Spicy Apricot Dipping Sauce. Serve potatoes hot with sauce. *Makes 6 servings*

Barbecue Chicken Sliders

1 pound ground chicken
½ cup barbecue sauce, divided
4 slices sharp Cheddar cheese, quartered (optional)
4 to 6 slices whole wheat sandwich bread
Lettuce leaves

1. Combine chicken and ¼ cup barbecue sauce in medium bowl. Shape mixture into 16 meatballs.

2. Spray large skillet or nonstick grill pan with nonstick cooking spray; heat over medium-high heat. Place meatballs in skillet; press with spatula to form patties. Cook patties 6 minutes per side or until cooked through (165°F). Top with cheese, if desired.

3. Meanwhile, toast bread. Cut into circles or quarters.

4. Top bread with lettuce and patties; serve with remaining barbecue sauce. *Makes 16 servings*

Ortega® Hot Poppers

1 can (3½ ounces) ORTEGA® Whole Jalapeños, drained
1 cup (4 ounces) shredded Cheddar cheese
1 package (3 ounces) cream cheese, softened
¼ cup chopped fresh cilantro
½ cup all-purpose flour
2 eggs, lightly beaten
2 cups cornflake cereal, crushed
Vegetable oil
ORTEGA® Salsa, any variety
Sour cream

CUT jalapeños lengthwise into halves; remove seeds.

BLEND Cheddar cheese, cream cheese and cilantro in small bowl. Place 1 to 1½ teaspoons cheese mixture into each jalapeño half; chill for 15 minutes or until cheese is firm.

DIP each jalapeño half in flour; shake off excess. Dip in eggs; coat with cornflake crumbs.

ADD vegetable oil to 1-inch depth in medium skillet; heat over high heat for 1 minute. Fry jalapeños, turning frequently with tongs, until golden brown on all sides. Remove from skillet; drain on paper towels. Serve with salsa and sour cream. *Makes 8 servings*

Parmesan Honey Lager Burgers

1½ pounds ground beef

¾ cup honey lager, divided

⅓ cup grated Parmesan cheese

1 tablespoon Worcestershire sauce

¼ teaspoon black pepper

3 tablespoons mayonnaise

3 tablespoons ketchup

½ teaspoon prepared mustard

8 slices tomato

8 thin slices red onion

4 hamburger buns

1. Prepare grill for direct cooking.

2. Combine beef, ¼ cup lager, Parmesan, Worcestershire sauce and pepper in medium bowl. Shape mixture into 4 patties. Combine 1 tablespoon lager, mayonnaise, ketchup and mustard in small bowl; set aside.

3. Grill patties over medium heat 3 minutes. Turn patties and brush with some of remaining lager. Grill 3 minutes more; turn patties and brush with lager. Repeat grilling and brushing 3 more times or until patties are cooked through (160°F).

4. Place 2 tomato slices, 2 onion slices and 1 burger on bottom halves of buns. Top with mayonnaise mixture and top halves of buns.   *Makes 4 servings*

Tipsy Chicken Wraps

1 tablespoon dark sesame oil

1 pound ground chicken

8 ounces firm tofu, diced

½ red bell pepper, diced

3 green onions, sliced

1 tablespoon minced fresh ginger

2 cloves garlic, minced

½ cup Asian beer

⅓ cup hoisin sauce

1 teaspoon hot chili paste

½ cup chopped peanuts

2 heads Boston lettuce, separated into large leaves

Whole fresh chives

1. Heat oil in large skillet over medium heat. Brown chicken, stirring to break up meat. Add tofu, bell pepper, green onions, ginger and garlic; cook and stir until onions are softened. Add beer, hoisin sauce and chili paste; cook until heated through. Remove from heat; stir in peanuts.

2. Place spoonful of chicken mixture in center of each lettuce leaf. Roll up to enclose filling. Wrap chives around filled leaves and tie to secure.

Makes about 20 servings

Oven-Fried Chicken Tenders

¾ cup vegetable oil

1 cup buttermilk

1 egg, beaten

1 cup all-purpose flour

2 to 3 teaspoons Cajun seasoning

¾ teaspoon paprika

½ teaspoon garlic powder

1½ pounds chicken tenders

Salt and black pepper

1. Pour oil into large roasting pan; place pan in cold oven. Preheat oven to 425°F.

2. Whisk buttermilk and egg in medium bowl until well blended. Combine flour, Cajun seasoning, paprika and garlic powder in shallow baking dish or pie plate. Coat chicken with flour mixture. Dip into buttermilk mixture; coat again with flour mixture. Place on plate in single layer. (If chicken begins to absorb flour, coat with flour mixture again.)

3. Place coated chicken in heated oil in roasting pan. Bake 6 minutes. Turn; bake 6 minutes more or until chicken is golden and cooked through. Place chicken on serving platter; season with salt and pepper.

Makes 6 to 8 servings

Sloppy "Cup of Joe" Sliders

1 tablespoon vegetable oil

1 small onion, halved and sliced

1 small green bell pepper, halved and sliced

1½ pounds ground beef

1½ cups spicy barbecue sauce (not mesquite)

½ cup ketchup

1 teaspoon instant coffee granules

1 package (16½ ounces) sweet Hawaiian dinner rolls

½ cup shredded Monterey Jack cheese

1. Heat oil in large skillet over medium heat. Add onion and pepper; cook and stir about 10 minutes or until softened but not browned. Remove from pan; set aside.

2. Brown beef in same skillet. Drain fat; return beef to skillet. Stir in barbecue sauce, ketchup and coffee granules. Reduce heat to medium-low; simmer 10 minutes.

3. Slice dinner rolls in half. Place about ⅓ cup sloppy joe mixture on bottom halves of rolls. Top with 1 tablespoon cheese and ¼ cup onions and peppers. Top with top halves of rolls; microwave on HIGH 15 seconds or until cheese is melted.

Makes 10 sandwiches

Cheesy Chicken Nachos

2 tablespoons olive oil

1 onion, diced

1 teaspoon POLANER® Chopped Garlic

1 pound ground chicken

1 jar (16 ounces) ORTEGA® Salsa, any variety, divided

2 teaspoons dried parsley

1 teaspoon ORTEGA® Chili Seasoning Mix

1 teaspoon REGINA® Red Wine Vinegar

½ cup water

12 ORTEGA® Yellow Corn Taco Shells, broken

1 pound shredded taco cheese blend (4 cups)

1 can (15 ounces) JOAN OF ARC® Black Beans

1 jar (12 ounces) ORTEGA® Sliced Jalapeños

HEAT oil in skillet over medium-high heat until hot. Add onion and garlic. Cook and stir until onion is translucent, about 3 minutes. Stir in chicken, ¾ cup salsa, parsley, seasoning mix, vinegar and ½ cup water; cook until meat is cooked through and sauce begins to thicken, about 5 minutes.

PREHEAT broiler; place rack about 7 inches from top of oven.

ASSEMBLE nachos by arranging broken taco shells on baking sheet. Sprinkle on 2 cups cheese; top with chicken mixture, black beans and jalapeños. Add remaining salsa and cheese. (If desired, prepare individual portions by dividing recipe among 6 heat-resistant plates.)

PLACE under broiler 4 minutes or until cheese begins to melt.   *Makes 6 servings*

Note: Be sure to have some of your favorite guacamole, sour cream and black olives on hand to place on top of the nachos.

Prep Time: 10 minutes • Start to Finish Time: 20 minutes

TIP

If you have ground beef on hand, you can still make these tasty nachos. Just brown the meat first and discard the excess fat before proceeding as directed. Or try this recipe with ground turkey.

Chicken Satay Skewers

6 garlic cloves, chopped

4 teaspoons dried coriander

4 teaspoons light brown sugar

2 teaspoons salt

1½ teaspoons HERSHEY'S Cocoa

1 teaspoon ground black pepper

½ cup soy sauce

6 tablespoons vegetable oil

2 tablespoons lime juice

4 teaspoons fresh chopped ginger

2½ pounds boneless, skinless chicken breasts

Peanut Dipping Sauce (page 89)

¼ cup fresh cilantro, chopped (optional)

1. Combine garlic, coriander, brown sugar, salt, cocoa and pepper in large bowl. Stir in soy sauce, oil, lime juice and ginger.

2. Cut chicken into 1½- to 2-inch cubes. Add to soy sauce mixture, stirring to coat chicken pieces. Cover; marinate in refrigerator for at least 2 hours.

3. Meanwhile, prepare Peanut Dipping Sauce. Thread chicken pieces onto skewers. Grill or broil, basting with marinade. Discard leftover marinade. Garnish with chopped cilantro, if desired. Serve with Peanut Dipping Sauce. Refrigerate leftovers.

Makes 15 to 20 appetizers or 4 to 6 entrée servings

Pizza Fries

1 bag (2 pounds) frozen French fries

1 cup PREGO® Traditional Italian Sauce, any variety

1½ cups shredded mozzarella cheese (about 6 ounces)

Diced pepperoni (optional)

1. Prepare the fries according to the package directions. Remove from the oven. Pour the sauce over the fries.

2. Top with the cheese and pepperoni, if desired.

3. Bake for 5 minutes or until the cheese is melted.

Makes 8 servings

Prep Time: 20 minutes • Bake Time: 5 minutes

Dips & SPREADS

Velveeta® Spicy Buffalo Dip

1 pound (16 ounces)
 VELVEETA®
 Pasteurized Prepared
 Cheese Product, cut
 into ½-inch cubes

1 cup BREAKSTONE'S®
 or KNUDSEN®
 Sour Cream

¼ cup cayenne pepper
 sauce for Buffalo
 wings

¼ cup KRAFT® Natural
 Blue Cheese
 Crumbles

2 green onions, sliced

Combine VELVEETA®, sour cream and pepper sauce in large microwaveable bowl. Microwave on HIGH 5 minutes or until VELVEETA® is completely melted, stirring after 3 minutes.

Stir in remaining ingredients.

Serve hot with celery and carrot sticks.

Makes 2¾ cups (22 servings)

Variation: Prepare as directed, using VELVEETA® Made With 2% Milk Reduced Fat Pasteurized Prepared Cheese Product and BREAKSTONE'S® Reduced Fat or KNUDSEN® Light Sour Cream.

Serve It Cold: This dip is also great served cold. Prepare as directed; cool. Cover and refrigerate several hours or until chilled. Serve as directed.

Keeping It Safe: Hot dips should be discarded after sitting at room temperature for 2 hours or longer.

Prep Time: 5 minutes • Total Time: 10 minutes

Asian Honey Mustard Dressing

¾ cup mayonnaise

2 tablespoons rice wine vinegar

2 tablespoons honey

2 tablespoons prepared mustard

1 teaspoon soy sauce

1 teaspoon dark sesame oil

Combine mayonnaise, vinegar, honey, mustard, soy sauce and oil in medium bowl; mix well.

Makes 1 cup dressing

Barbecue Dipping Sauce

1 can (15 ounces) **CONTADINA**® **Pizza Sauce**

¼ cup firmly packed brown sugar

2 tablespoons vinegar

1 tablespoon prepared mustard

½ teaspoon liquid smoke

1. Combine pizza sauce, brown sugar, vinegar, mustard and liquid smoke in medium saucepan.

2. Bring to a boil. Reduce heat to low; simmer, uncovered, for 5 minutes, stirring occasionally. Serve with chicken nuggets, meatballs, shrimp or cocktail franks, if desired. *Makes about 2 cups*

Prep Time: 3 minutes • Cook Time: 5 minutes

Creamy Cool Dipping Sauce

⅔ **cup mayonnaise**

¼ **cup ranch-style salad dressing**

3 **ounces crumbled feta cheese**

2 **teaspoons finely chopped green onion**

Combine mayonnaise and salad dressing in small bowl. Stir in cheese and green onion. Cover and refrigerate until ready to serve.   *Makes about 1¼ cups sauce*

Spicy Apricot Dipping Sauce

1 **cup apricot jam**

¼ **cup orange juice**

1 **tablespoon prepared mustard**

¼ **teaspoon ground red pepper**

Melt jam in small saucepan over medium-high heat. Whisk in orange juice, mustard and red pepper. Process in food processor or with immersible blender until smooth.   *Makes about 1¼ cups sauce*

Tip This sauce can be served with chicken as a dipping sauce, or brushed over cooked chicken and browned briefly under the broiler for a tasty glaze.

Buttermilk Ranch Dressing

¾ **cup mayonnaise**

½ **cup buttermilk**

2 **tablespoons chopped fresh chives**

1 **tablespoon chopped fresh parsley**

1 **clove garlic, minced**

1 **teaspoon salt**

½ **teaspoon black pepper**

Whisk mayonnaise, buttermilk, chives, parsley, garlic, salt and pepper in medium bowl. Refrigerate 30 minutes before serving.   *Makes 1¼ cups dressing*

Tip: This dressing can be made with whatever fresh herbs you have on hand, such as fresh cilantro, basil or thyme. If you don't have fresh herbs, use a smaller amount of dried.

Peach Dipping Sauce

½ **cup peach preserves**

2 **tablespoons light corn syrup**

1 **teaspoon white vinegar**

¼ **teaspoon ground ginger**

¾ **teaspoon soy sauce**

Combine preserves, corn syrup, vinegar and ginger in small saucepan. Cook and stir over medium-high heat until mixture simmers. Remove from heat; add soy sauce. Cool to room temperature.

Makes ½ cup sauce

Cucumber-Yogurt Sauce

1 container (7 ounces)
   plain Greek-style
   yogurt

½ seedless cucumber,
   peeled and grated

1½ tablespoons chopped
   fresh mint

1 tablespoon lemon juice

1 clove garlic, minced

   Salt and black pepper

Combine yogurt, cucumber, mint, lemon juice, garlic, salt and pepper in medium bowl until well blended. Cover; refrigerate until ready to serve.

Makes about 1¼ cups sauce

Peanut Dipping Sauce

½ cup peanut oil

1 cup REESE'S® Creamy
   Peanut Butter

¼ cup lime juice

¼ cup soy sauce

3 tablespoons honey

2 garlic cloves, minced

1 teaspoon cayenne
   pepper

½ teaspoon hot pepper
   sauce

Gradually whisk peanut oil into peanut butter in medium bowl. Blend in lime juice, soy sauce, honey, garlic, cayenne pepper and hot pepper sauce. Adjust flavors to taste for a sweet/hot flavor.

Makes 2¼ cups

Zesty Blue Cheese Dip

½ cup blue cheese salad
    dressing

¼ cup sour cream

2 teaspoons *Frank's®*
    RedHot® **Original**
    Cayenne Pepper Sauce

Combine dressing, sour cream and *Frank's® RedHot®* Sauce in medium serving bowl; mix well. Garnish with crumbled blue cheese, if desired.   *Makes ¾ cup dip*

Yogurt Chutney Dipping Sauce

½ cup plain yogurt

3 tablespoons mango,
    finely chopped

1 tablespoon cilantro,
    minced

1 tablespoon green onion,
    minced

¼ teaspoon hot sauce

⅛ teaspoon salt

In medium bowl, combine yogurt, mango, cilantro, onion, hot sauce and salt; cover and refrigerate until needed.   *Makes about ¾ cup sauce*

Favorite recipe from **National Chicken Council**

ACH Food Companies, Inc.

Campbell Soup Company

Delmarva Poultry Industry, Inc.

Del Monte Foods

The Hershey Company

©2009 Kraft Foods, KRAFT, KRAFT Hexagon Logo, PHILADELPHIA AND PHILADELPHIA
Logo are registered trademarks of Kraft Foods Holdings, Inc. All rights reserved.

VELVEETA is a registered trademark of Kraft Foods

Mrs. Dash® SALT-FREE SEASONING BLENDS

National Chicken Council / US Poultry & Egg Association

National Turkey Federation

Ortega®, A Division of B&G Foods, Inc.

Reckitt Benckiser Inc.

Tyson Foods, Inc.

MetricCHART

VOLUME MEASUREMENTS (dry)

⅛ teaspoon = 0.5 mL
¼ teaspoon = 1 mL
½ teaspoon = 2 mL
¾ teaspoon = 4 mL
1 teaspoon = 5 mL
1 tablespoon = 15 mL
2 tablespoons = 30 mL
¼ cup = 60 mL
⅓ cup = 75 mL
½ cup = 125 mL
⅔ cup = 150 mL
¾ cup = 175 mL
1 cup = 250 mL
2 cups = 1 pint = 500 mL
3 cups = 750 mL
4 cups = 1 quart = 1 L

VOLUME MEASUREMENTS (fluid)

1 fluid ounce (2 tablespoons) = 30 mL
4 fluid ounces (½ cup) = 125 mL
8 fluid ounces (1 cup) = 250 mL
12 fluid ounces (1½ cups) = 375 mL
16 fluid ounces (2 cups) = 500 mL

WEIGHTS (mass)

½ ounce = 15 g
1 ounce = 30 g
3 ounces = 90 g
4 ounces = 120 g
8 ounces = 225 g
10 ounces = 285 g
12 ounces = 360 g
16 ounces = 1 pound = 450 g

DIMENSIONS

1/16 inch = 2 mm
⅛ inch = 3 mm
¼ inch = 6 mm
½ inch = 1.5 cm
¾ inch = 2 cm
1 inch = 2.5 cm

OVEN TEMPERATURES

250°F = 120°C
275°F = 140°C
300°F = 150°C
325°F = 160°C
350°F = 180°C
375°F = 190°C
400°F = 200°C
425°F = 220°C
450°F = 230°C

BAKING PAN SIZES

Utensil	Size in Inches/Quarts	Metric Volume	Size in Centimeters
Baking or Cake Pan (square or rectangular)	8×8×2	2 L	20×20×5
	9×9×2	2.5 L	23×23×5
	12×8×2	3 L	30×20×5
	13×9×2	3.5 L	33×23×5
Loaf Pan	8×4×3	1.5 L	20×10×7
	9×5×3	2 L	23×13×7
Round Layer Cake Pan	8×1½	1.2 L	20×4
	9×1½	1.5 L	23×4
Pie Plate	8×1¼	750 mL	20×3
	9×1¼	1 L	23×3
Baking Dish or Casserole	1 quart	1 L	—
	1½ quart	1.5 L	—
	2 quart	2 L	—